33 POEMS AT 33

33 POEMS AT 33

And Other Works

W.J. LOUIS

CONTENTS

First Printing, 2022

For Kourtnie

PART 1

There's a fierce resolve
In the way
This once-worn ring waits,
But perhaps
Imprudently, for
One to place
Faith in its aplomb

PART 2

CHAPTER II

That day I learned a
New language
Through your little heart
Signaling
The whole of time, the
Unfolding
Of love's boundlessness

When you were a new-
Born, I fed
You poetry, bathed
You in dance
To the souls of jazz
Musicians,
Your head in my arms

CHAPTER IV

What is it that you
Dream of while
Nestled between your
Mother and
Me? I pray that you
Will never
Share my loneliness

CHAPTER V

Exoskeleton
Of a black
Insect pressed between
Two pages,
Punctuating old
Words with new
Interpretations

CHAPTER VI

Slithering down from
An upper-
Most branch outside our
Closed window:
A convoluted
Question posed
But insoluble

CHAPTER VII

I hear the laughter
Of children
As shadows lengthen
And enclose
Me in dark corners.
Must I leave
To be here for you?

CHAPTER VIII

Forgive me for my
Selfishness,
For fracturing our
Home, causing
Your lively smile to
Slip away
Amid your childhood

CHAPTER IX

Removing each book,
One by one,
From the confines of
Structured space;
The increasingly
Emptied shelves
Reflect my wet face

PART 3

CHAPTER X

Migrating eastward,
Clouds --- ghostlike ---
Imperturbably
Float round flecks
Of ethereal
Purple and
The droning of bees

CHAPTER XI

Old peaks beaten by
Thunderous
Clouds, today in dawn's
Lambency
Unveil full brilliance
Like elders
Bare tales for children

CHAPTER XII

A chorus of frogs,
Hidden in
Dampened hills, bedaubs
The humid
Darkness with an odd
And intense
Depth like a full moon

CHAPTER XIII

The stateliness of
A mother
Bear, conducting her
Ebon cubs
Across the coffee-
Colored eye
Of the observer

CHAPTER XIV

--- Swelling like oceans
Dextrously
Stroking the keys of
Their beaches ---
Bestriding the breath
Of summer ---
Shrill incantations

CHAPTER XV

An old tree, wearing
A glaucous,
Feathery mask of
Lichen, like
The eye socket of
A skull, peers
At me with one hole

CHAPTER XVI

The fluid poses
Of thin limbs
Sculpt pure light into
Angular
Beams, creating shade
Amid green
Leaves and white cascades

CHAPTER XVII

Neath dappled shadows
And the cold,
Plashing course of this
Stream adorned
With quick flashes of
Reflected
Rays lie smooth gray stones

CHAPTER XVIII

Sipping a silent
Melody
Neither unheard nor
Heard --- the taste
Of chrysanthemum
Buds reveals
The morning suchness

CHAPTER XIX

We share the same Mind
Underneath
All our grasping and
Rejecting;
Be the one who can
Forget such
Ills and drink with me

PART 4

CHAPTER XX

Our yearning for one
Another
Blooms on the stem of
Circumstance;
With shears in hand, we'll
Admire this
Time for its beauty

CHAPTER XXI

Before you and I
Stepped into
This shrine of breath that
Blows between
Us we removed our
Faces and
Planted them outside

CHAPTER XXII

The evening deepens
In our tea
Bowl of amber-hued
Hong cha; bright
Amid its smoky
Fragrance is
A red bean mochi

CHAPTER XXIII

You taste the years of
Longing for
Respite lingering
On my lips;
I respond to your
Chants at Love's
Altar and enter

CHAPTER XXIV

Suddenly orange
Afternoon
Sunlight --- lustily
Reflected
In lilting depths of
Birdsong: our
Kiss interrupted

CHAPTER XXV

"In another life,"
You say, "you
Were a mountain; I
Was a cloud,
Traveling across
The sky for
This sunset with you"

CHAPTER XXVI

I am enchanted
Amid your
Child-like playfulness:
Your movements
Speak like the numen
Of mountain
Forests; I listen

CHAPTER XXVII

I watch as you let
The rhythm
Of this old poem
Inhabit
You and enact its
Ardency
On your breath's passage

CHAPTER XXVIII

From windblown over-
Looks, lightning
Plunged into sight like
A diver
Over dark-clouded
Crests. We let
Go, outran the rain

CHAPTER XXIX

The creak of your soles'
Soft contact
With the floorboards of
The other-
Wise quiet Buddhist
Temple is
Loud --- and beautiful

CHAPTER XXX

You've found pleasure in
The colors
Of my passion and
A sense of
Belonging in all
The odd shapes
Of my character

CHAPTER XXXI

Nightfall fills our lungs,
Absorbs us
Into darkened-hours
Loudness and
Lights, the flavor of
Hojicha
Sweetening your tongue

CHAPTER XXXII

Enwrapped in your laugh
And these long
Tangles of whirling
Drunkenness:
Sake bottle's all
Empty; my
Rapture is swallowed

CHAPTER XXXIII

These hands, which molded
My mind with
Their own blood, beckoned
To you, clasped
Together with those
That pointed
Your way to my love

OTHER WORKS

Found Poem (from Emerson's Nature)

i
look
at
the
stars
come
from
stars
many
generations
come
out
of
the
universe
with
mind
open
to
the
flowers
the
animals
the

mountains
all
of
nature
the
presence
of
change
the
perfect
and
uncontained
immortal
by
thought
emotion
is
the
power
to
produce
in
man
it
is
the
spirit

Reflective

Scripture
Fixed
To
Her
Mirror
Outlines
An
Image

Heirloom

My
Creator
Conceived
A
Love
For
Her
God
Beseeched
His
Mercy
And
Evanesced
Into
The
Currents
Of
Change
A
Bubble
In
A
River
I
For
Years

Implored
Him
Then
To
Clear
My
Way
In
This
Wilderness
But
Found
The
Wild
To
Be
The
Absolute

Sundial

Childhood
Memories
Redolent
Of
Spontaneous
Freedoms
Warm
Simplicities
And
Otherworldly
Magic
Oddly
Warped
By
This
Deafening
Absence
Have
Thus
Far
Like
The
Headstone
Withstood
All
Comings

And
Goings
Of
The
Seasons
Which
Unheedingly
Burn
Our
Beautiful
Lives
Into
Oblivion

Snow Day

Crystalline
Blossoms
Cascade
Down
From
A
Dark
Limb

Finger Painting

The
Constellations
Are
Captured
And
Released
In
Our
Little
Hands
Streaking
Across
One
Open
Palm
Is
A
Shooting
Star

Humanity After Hughes

Preacher
Is
Poised
At
The
Pulpit
Loudly
Orating
On
Human
Nature
As
Sinful
Shouting
About
Our
Unworthiness
Bright
Cavorting
Light
Of
Late
Morning
Is

Obstructed
By
Stained
Glass
"He
Only
Asks
For
Ten
Percent
Of
Your
Hard
Earned
Honest
Income!"

School Night Moon

An
Outcast
Tear
Has
Disappeared
Into
Itself

Blues

I
Wonder
As
A
Heavy
Evening
Shower
Strums
The
Earth
If
The
Mantis
I
Released
Onto
The
Leaf
Outside
Our
Door
Has
Found
Repose
Amid
These

Dark
And
Dolorous
Airs

Cicadas

Like
Murmurs
Of
Ancestral
Incantations
Swelling
Like
Oceans
Dextrously
Stroking
The
Keys
Of
Their
Shores
Bestriding
Balmy
Breaths
Of
Summer
Galloping
Out
Of
A
Darkness

Sketch

Submersed
(Losing
All
Of
Me
In
You:
Dissolving)

The World After Basho

Slipping
From
My
Hands
Again
Eluding
Capture
Like
An
Evanescent
Dream
(Plash
!)

Ogre

That
Not
Yet
Oppressive
Orb
Illuminates
Script
Of
Harvested
Corn
A
Gaggle
Of
Geese
On
The
Ground
Forgo
For
A
While
A
Clouded
Sky

Autumnal

Shattered
Earthenware
Amid
Its
Grave
Of
Sticks
And
Bone
Dry
Leaves
Are
Strewn
Like
What
Remains
Of
Ancient
Enigmatic
Civilizations
But
A
Disentangled
Clump
Of
Soil

Has
Kept
Its
Potted
Shape
As
A
Surviving
Piece
Of
Culture
And
A
Precious
Little
Relic

Morning Glory

A
World
Unfolding
In
The
Choir
Of
Our
Garden

Untitled

Commune
With
The
Mountains
And
Feel
Their
Presence
Play
With
The
Stars
And
Hear
Them
Speak
Drink
With
The
Flowers
And
Smell
Their
Magic
Dance
With

The
Wind
And
Taste
Its
Spirit
Sit
With
The
Trees
And
Observe
Your
Mind

Appalachia in
Five Parts

I.

Sun
Glazed
Wading
Blithe
And
Resting
Climbing
Up
Bare
Drenched
Drifting
Pungent
Flitting
Over
Slick
Plummeting
Alter
Sonorous

II.

Majestic
Immense
Emergent
Swathed
In
Viridescent
Casting
Slate
Blue
Trickle
Through
Gnarled
Breaking
In
Refulgent
Whirling
Quietly
Pure
Providing

III.

Rhythmic
Thrown
Ablaze
Distant
Rising
Rotate
Changes
Polychromatic
Silencing
Slow
Traversing
Undisturbed
Receiving
Rolling
Resonant

IV.

Sweeping
Over
Forbidding
Blustery
Flinging
Fragrant
Across
Eerie
Jutting
Out
From
Shaded
Alluring
Lofty
Cover
Ancient
Calling

V.

Full
And
Lucent
Suffuses
Softly
Humming
Delicate
Dancing
Gracefully
Through
Inhaling
Participate
Idyllic
Arriving
Humbled
Returning